THE HEALED

The Healed: Timeless Lessons on the Healing Virtue of Christ

Copyright © 2020 The Jesus Center

All rights reserved. No part of this book may be used or reproduced by any means, graphic, electronic, mechanical, including photocopying, recording, taping, or by any information storage retrieval system without the written permission of the author except in the case of brief quotations embodied in critical articles and reviews.

Scriptures taken from the Holy Bible, New International Version®, NIV®. Copyright © 1973, 1978, 1984, 2011 by Biblica, Inc.™ Used by permission of Zondervan. All rights reserved worldwide. www.zondervan.com The "NIV" and "New International Version" are trademarks registered in the United States Patent and Trademark Office by Biblica, Inc.™

If no scripture reference is provided, PARA citation is used to indicate a paraphrasing by the author of the original source text.

ISBN: 9798627587578

A publication of Talll Pine Books

|| TALLPINEBOOKS.COM

*Printed in the United States of America

THE HEALED

THEO KOULIANOS SR.

Tall Pine

CONTENTS

Foreword	vii
Preface	ix
Introduction	xiii
1. Find Yourself in Him	1
Chapter One Study Questions	5
2. Desperation	7
Chapter Two Study Questions	11
3. His Own Received Him Not	13
Chapter Three Study Questions	19
4. He Carried It	21
Chapter Four Study Questions	27
5. Our Lord's Academy	29
Chapter Five Study Questions	39
6. Shedding Grave Clothes	41
Chapter Six Study Questions	47
7. He Opened Not His Mouth	49
Chapter Seven Study Questions	53
8. Just Love Him	55
Chapter Eight Study Questions	59
9. Have You Ever Seen Jesus?	61
Chapter Nine Study Questions	65
10. The Conclusion	67
Chapter Ten Study Questions	73
Meet the Author	75

Resources	77
Ministry Information	79
Suggested Scripture Reading	81
Notes	85

FOREWORD

Bookshelves across the world are filled with processes, steps, and methods to healing, wholeness, and recovery. Yet what has often lacked is not a *method* but a pure *motivation*. Systems don't necessarily birth hunger in the reader, but this book does. This unmatched work by Pastor Theo is a clarion call to compel the reader to the feet of Jesus, which is the starting line and the finish line for any and all healing.

The words herein are wrapped in bridal language. It's evident in reading *The Healed* that Pastor Theo has built a life filled with divine romance and a raw passion for the person of the Lord Jesus Christ. In this book, you'll find both guiding principles from the scriptures as well as remarkable modern accounts of miraculous healings by Christ.

If you or a loved one have need of healing, you

will find hope in this powerful book. Whether it's a new ailment or a chronic ailment, Pastor Theo makes clear that both are to be recipients of the chain-breaking power of God. This installment in the Global Discipleship Series is not only shedding the concept of healing in a good light, but most importantly shedding our Lord Christ Jesus in a good light. Pastor Theo is someone I admire and look up to in the Lord, and I encourage you to humbly receive the words our God has given him. You will be bettered by them both now and forever.

—Nicholas Poe, *Tall Pine Books*

PREFACE

There is a name that's above all names. When your body is stricken with disease, you need to know that there is a name above that disease. When you're bound to some addiction, there's a name above that bondage. When fear or poverty or loneliness attacks your soul, there is a name that eliminates that fear. There is a name that brings abundance. There is a name that brings peace. That name is *Jesus Christ of Nazareth.*

There is no other name but the name of Jesus Christ that could strike at the heart of the enemy and bring victory to our lives. There is power in the name of Jesus. There is a power that is beyond description that lies within the name of Jesus Christ; saturated in His love as no other name. Only the name of Jesus can heal you. Today, He alone is able to transform your sick body into a perfectly healed living temple, by the Holy Spirit. Jesus is healing. Jesus is our Healer. He healed 2,000 years ago and He is healing today. My prayer for this book is that the love and the power of the blood of His cross will raise your faith to a level that will appropriate the revelation of His power and love in your body and your life.

This I can tell you: over the last two or three decades, I have personally witnessed hundreds of miraculous healings. I have been privileged by the grace of God to see Jesus heal the blind, the deaf, the crippled, those riddled with cancer, those suffering from heart disease, skin disease, tumors, damaged backs, knees, and so, so much more. I have seen God take a tumor that was on a woman's breast and cause it to disappear within a matter of minutes. I've seen young children who were filled with the Holy Ghost manifest healing for the sick and deliverance for those that were afflicted. I have watched deliverance from sight problems, abdominal pain, mental disorders, and more. They have taken place in Greece, Brazil, India, Pakistan, Guatemala, Peru, and yes, at home in the United States, as well.

I've seen firsthand that there is nothing too difficult for Jesus and His name. His name is truly above all names! So my heart is that *The Healed* will take you on a journey of following the work of the Holy Spirit. I hope to reveal to you the things I've gleaned from those who have gone before me and the principles I've picked up from countless meetings, prayer sessions, and crusades. Above all, I want to share with you what I've learned and apprehended regarding the Word of God by the power of the Holy Spirit.

As you read this book, you will see time and time again how Jesus is the God that healed and still heals. Receive what is written in this book as a humble testimony of my heart directly to your heart, for the building of your faith; not faith in myself or anything else but the name of Jesus Christ of Nazareth. Jesus *will* deliver you, and He shall heal you of any and all diseases. This is *The Healed*.

INTRODUCTION

To you who are in pain and suffering from illness: it is time to be brought to the beautiful reality of the very love and power of Jesus Christ of Nazareth. There is love and power in both His body and His blood. God is coming to you; He brings with Him cords of love that He may wrap around your hearts. He presents to you a heart filled with compassion. He is ready to heal both your soul and your body. Your healing awaits you today in His divine, holy presence.

We need to tell the world through books such as this, "Let the epileptics, let the paralytic, let those who suffer and are tormented by demonic powers, let them all be set free by the power and the faith that is found only in the name of Jesus Christ of Nazareth. Everyone who was brought to Jesus Christ was healed 2,000 years ago. *Every single person*, regardless of their sickness, illness, or affliction was healed. And it must be the same today because Jesus Christ is the same yesterday, today, and forever (see Hebrews 13:8).

Jesus is the only answer and the divine remedy for freedom from sickness, addictions, and diseases. I once read in God's Word that a Roman officer came to see Jesus, asking for a miracle. He was saying, "Lord, I have a servant who is lying in my house, paralyzed and suffering terribly." Jesus replies to this Roman soldier and said, "I will go with you and I will heal him" (see Matthew 8).

Here you see a vivid truth. When Jesus said that He would go with the man, He was speaking of physically being present and utilizing His power to heal by direct contact. See, the power to heal is in His *presence*. From here, the conversation takes a turn. The man says, "All you need to do is command healing, send the word, and he will be healed."

Jesus looked at the man and was actually astonished when He heard his words. What then, does Jesus say? He said, "You have greater faith than anyone I have ever encountered in all of Israel." God's Word then says that Jesus turned to the officer and said to him, "Go home. All that you have believed for will be done for you." We then read that his servant was healed at that very moment.

If we come with the same expectant faith that this Roman centurion had, we too will see God's power. The sick are not healed by our own holiness, power, systems, methods, or programs. The sick are healed by faith in the name of Jesus. As that precious story in the gospels continues, we see that very evening, people brought many who were demonized to Jesus that He might speak a word of healing over them. They were all set free from torment and all manner of diseases were healed. God's unchanging will to heal continued to be displayed by Christ, through the Holy Spirit.

In Isaiah 53, God's Word declares, speaking prophetically about Jesus Christ, that He put upon Himself our weaknesses. In other words, *our wounds*. And He carried away our diseases and made us well. I ask you, did not massive crowds follow our Lord? Did not Jesus heal all who were sick? And, of course, we know the answer is *yes*.

Do you not recall when a man who had a demon, which made him both blind and unable to speak, was healed instantly by Jesus? The Bible says that crowds went wild with amazement. As a witness, the miracles we see in all of our meetings, gatherings, prayer circles, and crusades must point to Jesus and Jesus alone. We must let the world witness the glory, the power, and the love that is found only in God's Son, who obediently died upon the cross and then rose Himself up from the grave.

We can no longer quench the Holy Spirit from revealing Jesus to the Church and to the world, the

Bible says (see 1 Thessalonians 5:19). Following these healing encounters in Matthew 8, Jesus landed upon a shore and a huge crowd was waiting for Him. The importance of waiting for Jesus cannot be overstated. It is essential to knowing the grace of expectant faith to this very day. Jesus Christ is moved with the same compassion. When He sees the sick, the diseased, the afflicted, the oppressed, and the broken hearted—He is moved with the same compassion. His heart burns for you. We must continue with Him, waiting upon Him.

Yes, the waiting will, no doubt, cost you much and it can be painful, even lonely—but His loving heart will heal you, deliver you, and restore you. The Bible says massive crowds followed Him and He healed all who were sick (see Matthew 21:14). The blind and the crippled came into the temple courts, and Jesus healed them. Jesus healed in the temple. Jesus healed in the streets. Jesus healed in the wilderness. Jesus healed just one, and He healed the masses. Jesus healed the sinners and He healed the righteous. He healed nonbelievers so they would believe and healed the believers to galvanize their faith and provide much needed health to their bodies. What am I saying to you? Jesus Christ of Nazareth was and forever will be Lord and Savior of all who will call upon His name and who will come to Him by faith. Does not the Bible declare that blessings upon blessings come to those who love and trust Him?

There were no time constraints on His ministry meetings. He moved in the demonstration of the Spirit's power. That's what we are to do today by the power of the Spirit of Christ. Men, priests, rabbis, elders; none of them had control over Jesus' meetings. No board members, leadership, or special counsel directed the extent and nature of His meetings. He was empowered solely by the Holy Spirit. Nobody would dare to try to control or regulate His ministry. As a result, Jesus cured many who were sick with various diseases, and He cast out many demons.

But you see, Jesus would not permit the demons to speak, even though they tried. How many of us today are rejected by those within the Church? Possibly because they do not see what even the demons see. Remember, the demon said, "Christ, I know. Paul, I know. But who are you?" (see Acts 19).

The Bible tells us in Mark 3:7-10 that once again, Jesus withdrew to the lakeside with His disciples, but a massive crowd of people followed Him from all around the provinces of Galilee. Vast crowds came. Large numbers of people swarmed in from everywhere when they heard of Him and His wonderful works. Let this be so today! Let those who are reading this book, let those who are suffering, let those who need a healing touch swarm to Jesus today. If this book accomplishes anything, I want it to inspire you to seek Jesus and to hear Jesus. I long for you to witness the wonderful works of Christ.

We see that in Mark 3, Jesus gathers His disciples and is about to have a monumental moment with them. He appointed the 12 whom He named apostles. He wanted them to be continually at His side, witnessing and watching His works, that He may send them later to do the same. He gave them authority to cast out demons and heal the sick. When Christ set them in office as apostles, it was not a passive calling. He actively set them in place so His purpose and glory would be revealed. The Greek verb speaks of it with the word *poleo*, which speaks of doing or making.

In other words, Jesus imparted His divine favor, blessing, and grace upon them to see them in a place as His apostolic missionaries for the Kingdom. We know that the word apostle is a Greek word from *apostolos*, which speaks of being "sent out" by God. They were sent, and so are you. You are sent out as His ambassadors. He ordained them that they might accompany Him and then preach and demonstrate His love and power. At first, there were 12, then there were 70, and from there, the multiplication continued. None of them were ready. None of them were fully equipped. None of them were educated, for the Holy Spirit had not yet come. They were not empowered divinely. None of them were prepared because Jesus had not yet been glorified. My heart is that the leaders of today will realize that they need to raise up others and that they can no longer just center their ministry work around themselves. They are to choose certain individuals and then pour into their hearts. And this is solely the work of the Holy Spirit. The legacy of a spiritual father is made up of those whom He has released and sent forth to proclaim Christ into the world. That is the inheritance of the Kingdom. Healing, miracles, and the preaching of the Word is not merely to be received by the crowd but accomplished through the crowd. May God raise up more and more of His servants to carry out the commission.

1

FIND YOURSELF IN HIM

The healing of the sick is not merely some theological or academic subject. Healing the sick is who Jesus is and what Jesus does. He is both Lord and Savior, not only of our souls, but of our bodies, as well. There's a tendency, it seems, as we grow in the Lord, to hunger and to know more about the healing grace of God or to seek a system, method, doctrine, or some steps to follow to be healed or to pray for the sick. Yet healing the sick is not a system.

Yes, we can, with pure motives, attempt to create atmospheres in our meetings that would be more conducive to revealing the healing grace of God among the sick. But we need to be at rest and at peace, for the rest that we seek for afflicted bodies and souls is to be found only in Jesus Christ. There is an old saying when one is buying real estate that goes: *location, location, location is everything*! But in the Kingdom of God, that is not so. When it comes to the Kingdom of God and the King Himself, He is not limited to any specific location chosen by man to heal the sick. Yes, we can find scriptures where God has determined a certain place in which He chooses to manifest His glory, His power, and the essence of who He is. But Jesus is by no means restricted to the power or the gifts of men.

See, to those being healed in the Bible, the only location issue was simply finding where Jesus was. Why? Because there's no better location where one of us can experience Jesus and His grace of healing than that place where Jesus has chosen to manifest His presence. We see in the gospels that Christ would heal, move on down the road, heal more, move down the road, and heal again. The crowds followed, faith followed, and healing manifested. Jesus was the divine meeting point between God and man. In other words, at the presence of the Lord Himself, the sick were healed.

The people did not come for some great religious experience or some great gathering of people. They came for one purpose: that they may be healed and set free in the presence of the Lord. Let us apprehend what happened. People came to Jesus and Jesus healed them. This is the pure and simple result of people flocking to meet Christ. You might ask, *how can I come to Jesus when He is not physically present?* I say to you, you can find yourself in His very presence by opening up His very Word. When the Word comes into your heart, the Spirit works Himself through every fiber of your being—body included. The scriptures declare that the words of God are "Life to those who find them and health to one's whole body" (see Proverbs 4:22).

As you submerge your heart in His Word, His presence will encompass you. Healing will be found. The multitudes knew how to seek out Christ's presence. As they did, they continued with Him for days, often without food or drink. The scriptures are explicitly clear that Jesus had compassion on them. Oh, what a gift the Lord's compassion is in our lives! Imagine, these sick, poor people continued with Jesus with no food, no shelter, no comforts in the pain and suffering of their condition. The Lord continued on in this incredible healing service in the place He chose to host it. His three-day healing crusade was this lonely mountainside without food or water or the comforts of life. It was simple: in attendance were the sick, lame, blind, and diseased, and Jesus Christ. That's all that was needed. His disciples were there to watch and to do as He said.

In that place, the sick obtained their healing. They knew in their hearts that Jesus was their only hope and that Jesus was the medicine they needed to be made whole. Who could ever imagine what that scene must have looked like? Sitting on a mountainside was the Son of God, and at His feet were multitudes of sick and afflicted men, women, and children. It's safe to say this could not have been an orderly meeting as we are accustomed to today in our churches and conferences.

The people continued with the Lord and would not depart from that hillside. They refused to leave in the same condition they had come. Now there are some, I'm sure, who had to be carried there. The blind had to be led, but it did not matter. All had one common mission: *get to Jesus*. It always comes down to get to Jesus. Get to Him. He is the answer. Your hope rests in Him. So I say to you who are reading this book, Jesus Christ is most certainly the same yesterday, today, and forever. He changes not.

CHAPTER ONE
STUDY QUESTIONS

1) Have your found yourself reducing healing to an academic subject? How can you avoid this?

___

2) What can you learn from the life of Jesus about God's will toward those who are afflicted?

___

3) Those who were desperate did all they could do to get to Jesus. What does that look like in our modern world?

___

Additional thoughts:

2
DESPERATION

"Praise the Lord, my soul; all my inmost being, praise his holy name. Praise the Lord, my soul, and forget not all his benefits—who forgives all your sins and heals all your diseases." (Psalm 103:1-3)

God's Word declares in this opening line that "With my whole heart, with my whole life, with my innermost being, I bow and wonder in love before the holy God. My Lord, You are my soul celebration. How can I forget the miracles of kindness You have done for me? You have kissed my heart with forgiveness. In spite of all that I have done, Jesus, your kiss is forgiveness. For You have healed me inside and out from every disease. You have rescued me from hell and saved my life!" Amazing, isn't it? God's Word says that He kisses us with forgiveness and He has healed us inside and out from every disease.

Psalm 6:2 declares, "Please deal gently with me. Lord, show me your mercy. For I am sick and frail. I am fading away from weakness. Heal me, for I am falling apart." In the church, we need to put aside some of the concepts and ideas we have generated in the faith—one of them being the idea that we cannot beg and cry out to God. Some subscribe to the idea that we have to act neat and orderly, unable to cry out from pain. Yet this is not the pattern of scripture. It's okay to cry out to the Lord or even beg Jesus for His mercy. David begged the Lord to be saved and healed. God responds to our outcry and desperation.

It's okay to get down on your knees and face before the Lord from the depths of your heart, in the midst of your pain, and cry out to Jesus. He loves you. What Father does not want to embrace and pull into His bosom His child? He longs to hold you close to reveal the depth of His love by the healing of your body. Our God is worthy of our outcry. Our God is better than anyone you could ever hope or imagine. There is nobody like Jesus. Psalm 107 talks about how they cried out to the Lord in their trouble and He delivered them from all of their destructions. The psalm goes on to talk about how God changes our wilderness into a pool of living water. Friends, Jesus makes the hungry heart to dwell in His presence. He changes our dry land into springs of water. And so today, my prayer is that you will experience, even as you're reading this, His beautiful, holy presence.

Often, we get so caught up in formulas that we forget that the healing of the sick occurs when our loving God simply envelopes us in His arms, far away from sickness and affliction. Jesus Christ of Nazareth longs to gather you as His sheep into His bosom. His love cries out. He implores us to come to Him, and as we do, we find rest. Our rest-source has not changed. We once wandered in the wilderness with no direction or dwelling place. Our spirits thirsted for satisfaction, yet we found none in sin. Our staggering souls were filled with weakness and despair. Yet we cried out to God, and He helped us. He rescued us. He led us by His nail scarred, loving hands to a place of health and safety. He will do it again. His mind has not changed on the matter. It's settled for all of eternity.

Jesus has shattered the steel bars that have held us back from our healings, from our restoration to our deliverance, and beyond. We must remember His promise: "Many are the afflictions of the righteous. But Jesus Christ of Nazareth has delivered us from all of them" (see Psalm 34). God is love. His blood is filled with His love. His blood is our heavenly remedy for every sickness and sin. His blood is God's divine medicine against all disease. His blood is God's antidote against all sin, all disease, all torments, and even death itself.

Let us go out and preach His gospel, teach of His kingdom, and heal the sick. For this is what Jesus has called us to do. The Holy Spirit is waiting to reveal and to affirm the gospel of Jesus Christ and the kingdom of God in us and through us. He does so by healing the sick and by destroying every evil yoke of the enemy. The fame of Him shall be spread abroad. So let us give Him our hearts to dwell in, for He has given us His.

CHAPTER TWO
STUDY QUESTIONS

1) The chapter begins with a passage from Psalm 103. In what ways does the 103rd psalm inspire you? How does it apply to your life now?

_____
_____
_____
_____
_____

2) Have you ever truly cried out to God in desperation? What was the result?

_____
_____
_____
_____

3) The chapter speaks of our need to cry out to God in desperation when we have need of healing and deliverance. What harmful impact comes about when we abandon the true healing message and cling to formulas instead?

_____
_____
_____
_____

Additional thoughts:

3

HIS OWN RECEIVED HIM NOT

"A large crowd followed and pressed around him. And a woman was there who had been subject to bleeding for twelve years. She had suffered a great deal under the care of many doctors and had spent all she had, yet instead of getting better she grew worse. When she heard about Jesus, she came up behind him in the crowd and touched his cloak, because she thought, 'If I just touch his clothes, I will be healed.'" (Mark 5:24-28)

This suffering woman was at the end of her rope. She had tried everything and nothing was working. In her weakness and desperation, she pressed in to get to Jesus. When she touched His clothes, the blood dried and her body was immediately and totally healed! Christ had many people around Him. People were touching Him and striving for His attention. In the midst of the chaos, He sensed a touch that was different. The Bible says, "At once Jesus realized that power had gone out from him. He turned around in the crowd and asked, 'Who touched my clothes?'" (Mark 5:30). The disciples heard this and probably thought...*everyone here is trying to touch You. What do You mean?*

Yet this was different. He perceived the demand she had placed on His love and anointing to heal. She came forward to the feet of Jesus. Their eyes met at that very moment. This woman who had suffered for years was now face to face with Jesus, the Son of God. Jesus said to her with His loving voice, "Daughter, your faith has made you well. Go in peace and be healed of your affliction." This is His character. It's His nature. This was not an isolated incident.

S*ozo* is a Greek word which speaks of life, safety, soundness, healing, deliverance, wholeness, rescue restoration, and salvation. It has been translated as the simple English word "saved." Yet it encompasses so much more. Jesus is *sozo*. He is our safety, soundness, healing, wholeness, restoration, and salvation. That is who Jesus is and so much more. Even though hundreds of people pressed against His body as the Lord walked through these crowds, only one poor, suffering woman got His attention. She touched Jesus with all her heart and with divine faith. And she came to that place where she knew that Jesus was all that she needed because Jesus was all that she had left. There is a saying that I've heard many times before: you will know that Jesus is all you need when Jesus is all you have.

So settle it deep in your hearts: Jesus healed all who came to Him 2,000 years ago as He walked among His creation. Do not let anyone lead you astray; there is no one like Jesus Christ of Nazareth. As we trek through the gospels, we come across Mark 6:1-5, where Jesus returned to His home town. It was the day of Sabbath, meaning rest. As was His custom, He went into the synagogue to teach. The people were amazed at His teaching for He taught with authority. They saw His mighty works and were dumfounded. The only thing they managed to utter was, "Is this not Jesus, the son of the carpenter?" In other words, "Isn't this the guy from down the street? How is He teaching with such revelation?"

Their astonishment turned to offense, and the people began to reject Him. The prophecy would prove to be true that He would come to His own, and His own would not receive Him. In fact, it caused Him to say, "A prophet is not without honor, except in his home town, among his friends and relatives" (Mark 6:4).

I am sure many of you can relate to Jesus in this instance. He was experiencing persecution and rejection from those He loved. All He desired in His heart was that they be set free from their slavery to sin and sickness. The most tragic result is the hardness of their hearts. Maybe you've experienced your friends, family, or relatives creating an atmosphere of dishonor. And they cast you out from among them in their hearts; the outcome to their souls and their bodies will only be known one day before God. The fellowship of the sufferings of Christ Jesus includes dishonor. There are no exceptions to this in that place of dishonor. Often God may choose to not do any great miracles. He may heal just a few sick people by laying hands upon them, even though His heart was and is to heal *all* who are sick (Mark 6:5).

Please allow me to speak openly to you, the Church. My words are saturated with love, and nothing more. I implore you, please do not look to dictate the ministry of God. This is not order. This is quenching the Holy Spirit of Christ, who is Lord over His Church. Just look for a moment at Jesus' heart and ministry. We see in Luke 4 at sunset, the people brought all those who were sick to Jesus to be healed. Jesus laid hands on them one by one, and they were all healed of different ailments and sicknesses. Time was of no concern when Jesus ministered. Jesus would continue with His ministry as the people continued with Him. This is so critical for the Church to apprehend in their hearts.

The most outcast people in society, in Jesus' day, were the lepers. For they were both spiritually and physically unclean. Now just imagine how foul they were, the foul smell that must have flowed out of their bodies. They had no clean clothing, ability to bathe properly, and they were quite literally unapproachable. Yet Jesus saw them as approachable and lovable.

One day, Jesus was ministering in a certain city. While in that certain city, it says in Luke 5:12 that the Lord chose to come upon one such man covered with leper sores. He was untouchable, hated, incurable, and hopeless. This man knew no peace, no love, no life; all who saw him fled from his presence. Certainly no one would think of embracing such a man. So this leper recognizes Jesus and he falls on his face, at the feet of the Lord.

He begged to be healed. There, on his face in total submission and desperation, he cried out. "If you are willing, you can completely heal me," he implored. Jesus was pierced to His heart by this man's desperate plea and his faith. And Jesus reached out and touched him, saying, "I am willing, be cleansed." You know what's amazing here? Jesus touched him first, then spoke to him. Suddenly, the leper sores were gone and they were healed, and his skin was smooth! News about what Jesus had done spread fast within the region. Massive crowds continued gathering.

This was the ministry of Jesus Christ, the Healer. This is the ministry of Jesus Christ to this very day. To Him belongs all power and authority to heal and deliver from every unclean ailment and from the grip of the evil one. Out of Jesus' presence is the power of Jesus revealed and manifested to all. Jesus seeks faith, a faith that believes in one's own heart. Just one word spoken from the Lord is all that is needed for anyone to be healed. One touch by one believing heart brings forth the healing of sickness, disease, and all demonic oppression.

CHAPTER THREE
STUDY QUESTIONS

1) The woman at the start of the chapter was at the end of her rope. She had no other options. Why does such a posture position her to receive from Jesus?

2) As we see in the chapter, the word *saved* is the greek word *sozo*. How does this full and complete definition change your view of the word *salvation*?

3) The chapter states that the ministry of Jesus continues to this very day. How have you seen the ministry of Christ Jesus work in and through your own life?

Additional thoughts:

4
HE CARRIED IT

"This was to fulfill what was spoken through the prophet Isaiah: 'He took up our infirmities and bore our diseases.'" (Matthew 8:17)

Imagine this: Jesus, the Son of God, choosing to bear cancer, arthritis, high blood pressure, AIDS, blindness, leprosy, palsy, epilepsy, and every other disease, germ, virus, or influenza you could conjure up. Why? *Love.* Out of His love, He did what He did. He has taken on what we deserved so that we could take on what He deserved. The great exchange of Calvary has taken place. He has done it all. All that is required on our part is to simply trust in what He did and what He does. When we do, we act on it. This is the greatest exchange in all of history!

It is said that in order for a gift from one person to another to be formalized, the beneficiary of the gift has to take possession of it. So it is up to you and me to take hold of the gift of the blood of the cross and to walk in the divine wellness of our soul and bodies. We know that one of Christ's redemptive names is Jehovah Rapha, meaning *the God that heals*. In Exodus 15, Israel had come out of bondage in Egypt. Their bodies must have been beaten up, arthritic, sore, bruised, and worn down. As a result, God chose to reveal Himself to them quite intentionally as *the God who heals*. According to Hebrews, we stand today in a better covenant built upon better promises. Imagine there was not one feeble among them, after 430 years in bondage!

The scriptures tell us in Mathew 9, as well as Acts 10, that Jesus went about healing in all the streets, cities, and villages around. By the Spirit, it's still happening among the people in every church, nation, and home around the world. Yet you might say, "How does one appropriate such healing?" God requires that the people of the world have faith in Him. Jesus simplified our directive when He said, "Have faith in God" (see Mark 11). He does, however, heal the unbelieving sick that they might believe. The name of Jesus Christ is far greater than ailments of any kind. Cancer has a name. Injuries have a name. Spine issues have a name. Yet the name of Jesus is far above any name!

See, God is giving ordinary people an extraordinary gift to see the sick healed, the crippled to walk, the blind to see, and people made whole. He is using our earthly hands to bring about divine works. Please allow me the honor to share with you about one such miraculous healing that I witnessed in my life with Christ the Healer. In this book, I testify of many healings by the Lord Jesus upon the peoples from many nations, both poor and rich alike.

One such healing took place in Pakistan via a Skype healing service. The Lord had me to minister to this particular group in 2018. This will most certainly astound you and increase your faith. As I was ministering via Skype to a group of poor pastors and missionaries in Pakistan, there was a point in that service that God gave me a word of knowledge, and it was totally divine. In the middle of my ministering, the Spirit spoke to my heart to stop preaching and to declare that there is a woman there who had a serious illness or problem in her womb. That was all. I did not perceive exactly what the problem was. I did not know in my own understanding, yet God revealed it to me.

And so I shared this revelation with the host pastor, the evangelist, and he and turned and shared that with those gathered and suddenly a woman came forward, testifying that she had a health issue in her womb. Now she did not give specifics, but in obedience to the Holy Spirit, I asked the pastor's wife to place her hand upon the woman's womb and to repeat my prayer to this dear lady in the dialect of the people, and she did.

The woman began to testify that she could feel something in her womb and her abdomen area, and then I proceeded to continue on with the meeting. A few hours later, after the Skype meeting was completed, I received a Skype call from the pastor. He told me that this woman was pregnant and that the baby she was carrying had been diagnosed as being dead by the doctors. For obvious reasons, the physicians wanted to remove the dead child by performing a medical procedure, yet this woman refused, and over a period of two weeks she carried this lifeless child in her womb, and this woman believed God would bring her child back to life.

Now, let me say clearly, I am not encouraging or promoting that if anyone is found in a similar situation, they neglect proper medical care. What I say is that they ought to seek proper medical attention and then, after careful consultation and prayer, decide what to do. However, she believed that she had to attend the Skype meeting that we were hosting. After a couple of days, I received another Skype call from the host pastor. He was absolutely ecstatic. He told me that the woman that I prayed for went back to her doctors to have the child removed.

But she asked one thing of the doctors, that they would do another test to be sure that the child was, in fact, dead and without life. The mother believed by faith that what she felt the day we prayed for her was God bringing her dead child back to life. The doctors performed some tests to see if there was a heartbeat. To their amazement, the baby had a heartbeat. This child, who was without a heartbeat and diagnosed dead, had come back to life. I remember some months later, the pastor and the woman and her husband made a Skype call to me. And there she was, holding her new precious infant in her arms. God had caused the dead, even in the womb with his mother, to be raised to life. This is just one testimony of hundreds of healings that I have witnessed God perform in the lives of so many people around the world. May you never forget that God will respond to your outcry and act when He sees your desperation.

CHAPTER FOUR
STUDY QUESTIONS

1) The chapter mentions that the beneficiary must take possession of that which is provided. What does it look like, practically speaking, to take possession of your healing?

_____
_____
_____
_____
_____

2) God requires that we have faith in order to receive healing. How can we cultivate this?

_____
_____
_____
_____
_____

3) The chapter lays out a powerful testimony from a Skype call. How does the testimony in this chapter inspire you to trust God for healing in your own life or in the lives of others?

_____
_____
_____
_____
_____

Additional thoughts:

5
OUR LORD'S ACADEMY

Allow me to share with you about our Lord's Academy, a school that was founded by the Holy Spirit through the faithful life of my wife, Evelyn. As our Lord's Academy grew from an enrollment of six students up to over 100, the incredible move of the Holy Spirit became more and more profound. Let me also say that all the glory goes to Jesus Christ of Nazareth for what I'm about to share with you. This is, in no way, intended to bring any honor, glory, or praise to the school, to the ministry, to my wife, for myself, or to our staff. Each of us were simply surrendered vessels unto the Lord by the leading of the Spirit of Christ.

That said, I truly can't remember how all of this divine work of the Holy Spirit got started. It just did. Jesus just began healing people who came to visit as the students and the staff would pray for them in the name of Jesus Christ. But I do remember an incredible miracle that occurred in the life of one of our students' grandmothers. She came to see me personally while the school was in session. We were standing outside one of the portable classrooms. She was a dignified woman, very soft spoken, and she approached me to share with me about this affliction she was dealing with.

If my memory serves me correctly, she told me that she was diagnosed with a golf ball sized tumor in the back of her head at the base of her brain. This wonderful Catholic woman who loved Jesus much came with an expectant faith in the love and power of the name of our Lord. I remember closing my eyes, asking the Holy Spirit to inspire my prayer. I do recall that I applied the blood of Christ upon my life and hers. I then confessed the healing promises of God upon her. Then, with a supernatural boldness, I commanded that tumor to leave her body.

God led me to call the principal of the school out from her classroom. The woman and I were standing there along with the principal who came and joined us. I shared with her that God wanted me to tell her that the grandmother would see the hand of God's love upon her. And before any of us knew by sight, I was confessing her healing before the doctors would even affirm it a few days later.

So later that week, the grandmother went back to the doctor for treatment, and she then returned to the school to give us a report. She said they found no tumor. Jesus Christ had again affirmed His gospel in a glorious way!

Many times throughout the day, we would receive calls from different people who were suffering from various illnesses. Some people would call on behalf of a family member or friend. We would stop all classes, the entire student body would come together, and we would call upon the name of Jesus and for His healing mercy to manifest. Testimony after testimony continued to come. For example, a woman named Sofia approached me one day for prayer. She was a regular in our morning chapel services. She told me that she had a disease she had been dealing with on her hands and that for many years she had seen many doctors and had various treatments and nothing would cure her.

I looked at her hands and my heart was stirred with compassion for her. Her hands were riddled with a disease and I could see how painful it must have been for her. And when I began waiting on the Holy Spirit to guide my prayer, I had a word in my heart from God regarding this matter. The Lord was telling my heart that I was to touch her hands with my hands. I told her this and she wept. She shared that no one had touched her hands, not even her husband, during that entire period of her affliction.

I was moved by faith. God spoke to me as I laid my hands directly upon her diseased hands in obedience to the leading of the Holy Spirit. I told her that God was speaking to my heart, and that in seven days, her hands would be totally clean. The worship service continued. The woman went her way. One week later, in the middle of one of our Sunday services during praise and worship, I saw Sofia entering the back of the chapel entrance. She stood in the back and raised her hands for me to see. As I looked, I suddenly realized that her hands were completely clean and perfect. God had once again done what only He could do!

Over a period of many years, miraculous healings occurred upon the small campus of our Lord's Academy and the children never doubted. It was settled that by His stripes, we are healed! For several weeks, I had been teaching at the school about the person of the Holy Spirit and the baptism of the Spirit. The children, ranging in ages from kindergarten to high school, learned of God, the Holy Spirit, and His anointing. Now, keep in mind, the students came from various religious beliefs, races, and cultures. Yet I knew in my heart that I had to reveal the truth of the gospel regarding a Spirit of God, His presence, and His power to these children.

For weeks, I cried out to God in my own private prayer time for Him to manifest Himself miraculously, because I did not want us to be some academic exercise. I wanted the children to experience, in their own lives, the reality of the Holy Spirit. In this,

His Word would come alive before their very eyes, and everything would change, both for the students and the staff.

One morning during our daily chapel service, as I was ministering on the Holy Spirit, God had me call all the students forward out of their chairs. And so they came and stood in front of me in one single line, all facing toward me, and we continued in worship and in prayer. All the children had their eyes closed and were truly fixing themselves on the presence of God and glorifying Him. I did not say a word. I waited on God. Suddenly, I heard one of the children begin to pray in the Spirit. This child was praying and worshipping God with a heavenly tongue.

Then, suddenly, others began doing the same. God descended into that chapel. All the children were praying and weeping. One of the children who happened to be deaf from birth began praying in tongues loudly. God was baptizing these children with His Spirit and fire. All of them received the baptism of the Holy Spirit, and from that day on, the school's reputation and fame of Jesus was set abroad.

The way that God began to move in the midst of these students became known in the community. Charisma magazine heard about what was going on in this little school of our Lord's Academy. It was literally affecting more people than we imagined. The local CBS News affiliate, as well, came and shot a couple specials on what was happening. Churches in New Hampshire, Michigan, Alabama, and Florida even began inviting us and the children to come to their churches to pray for the sick. Everywhere the children went, they proclaimed the gospel and God healed the sick through their lives. Doors began to open for many of our team to go out and to see God heal and set countless hurting people free.

Then the doors began to open for me to travel to Brazil with a good pastor friend of mine. As we went there to minister the gospel, this would prove to be God's launching pad to the nations in His power and for His glory. During my first trip to Brazil, we traveled to several cities over a period of 10 days, preaching the kingdom and healing the sick in His name. For me, it was a defining moment of my life as a man called to heal the sick in the name of Christ our Lord.

Now, after about 10 days of ministry and many services later, we finally had our last meeting, which was the night before coming back to United States. Pastor Abraham, the pastor who invited me, was a great prophet of the Lord and psalmist, and had a Word from God. God spoke to him that he was to call me forward, to begin praying for the sick and the blind. Keep in mind, I had never witnessed in my own presence a blind eye open, nor had I ever prayed for somebody that was blind. But as I was standing there at the altar, without any idea as to what I was to do, as I looked out among the hundreds gathered, I saw a woman being led to the front toward me. The closer she got to the front of the church, I knew that she could not see and was totally blind. As she came close to me. I could see her eyes were covered with a milky white-like substance. She was so frail and poor and desperate, my heart broke into a thousand pieces.

As I looked upon her without knowing what else to say, I asked her, "What do you want?" And she said, with such desperation, "I want to see." I was overwhelmed with the moment and I fell to my knees and began to weep. And I began asking, "God, I don't know what to do. What should I do?" Then softly, He spoke to my heart, "Stand up, anoint her eyes with oil, then tell everyone in the church when she opens her eyes, she will see."

I replied to the Lord, "What if this doesn't work and the people think I'm a fake?" Jesus gently rebuked me and commanded me to obey Him. It had nothing to do with me and everything to do with Him. And so I stood and I told the whole church assembly what I was going to do, and that when the woman opened her eyes, she would see. I can tell you, silence fell over that church. Every eye was fixed upon the front, on that woman and myself. So by faith in Jesus Christ, I anointed her eyes in the sign of a cross with the oil. And then I commanded that in the name of Jesus Christ of Nazareth, she be healed from this blindness, not knowing what to do or what to expect.

I asked the woman to open her eyes. I have to confess to you that it had to be the longest moment of my life. When she opened her eyes, she was squinting from the lights; and suddenly I realized: *why would a blind woman be bothered by the light?* Suddenly I realized that Jesus had miraculously given her sight. And so she began to cry out in her native tongue, "I can see, I can see!"

Pandemonium broke out in that church. As I looked to my right, I saw that five other blind people were helped to the front of the church. The power of God was truly present to heal without me saying one word to them. I didn't even go over to touch them. Within minutes God gave eye sight to these five also. I asked the Lord, "Why?" He said, "Because this is who I am."

Over the next many years, God would have me to return to Brazil, to declare the gospel and to heal the sick. On one of those occasions, I was asked by a local radio station to teach and pray for the city of Sorocaba, Brazil. Along with my interpreter, we went to the small radio station and they took us inside a recording booth. We were given 30 minutes to tell the city about Jesus and to pray for those who would be listening. In a matter of 30 minutes, let me tell you what happened. The phone calls began to come in. The phones rang and rang. So many calls were coming in that the volunteers had to go out and grab people and bring him back inside the station to answer the calls.

People were calling for prayer and many were testifying about what God had done. In less than 30 minutes, we had received over 120 testimonies of healings. God was truly invading a city by His power. We saw so many healings in the weeks, months, and years that followed us. Cancer, heart disease, deformed legs, healed blindness, deafness, skin disease; all were healed in the name of Jesus Christ of Nazareth.

CHAPTER FIVE
STUDY QUESTIONS

1) What can you learn from the way in which Pastor Theo ministers healing in the examples from this chapter?

_____
_____
_____
_____
_____

2) In the chapter, the Holy Spirit fell on the students in a mighty way. Yet before that, prayers for this sort of movement had been offered up in private. What is the connection between the two?

_____
_____
_____
_____
_____

3) God said, "This is who I am," in regard to healing the blind. What does this story tell you about the nature of God? What can be learned from it?

_____
_____
_____
_____
_____

Additional thoughts:

6
SHEDDING GRAVE CLOTHES

My dear brothers and sisters, all that I have shared in these previous chapters is to do the will of God and to reveal to you what Jesus has done so that you might believe in Him as your Lord, Savior, Healer, and Deliverer. In the midst of this, keep in your heart the reality that Jesus loves you. We are all entitled, as His children, to every blessing of His kingdom. He came to set us free from the curse of sin and death; and He came to save our souls and our bodies.

Jesus is the eternal Son of God who came to earth and lived among His people. Most of the people did not recognize who it was that lived among them walking, eating, drinking, sleeping, teaching, and preaching...it was God Himself. Thousands and thousands would come to find Him to hear Him and to see His miraculous works. He healed everyone who asked for it. All that the people needed to do was come to Him. Some had faith and were healed. Others who had little faith were healed, as well. This was done that they might believe in Him and the work of His cross.

Jesus gave up His Spirit willingly, but He did not do that until He was finished with the purpose for which He came. He had shed His precious and holy blood to destroy sin and the curse of sin. His blood redeemed us from Satan's grasp. Because of the power of His blood, sin could no longer enslave us. All of our iniquities were upon Him, and He exchanged His holy life so we may have His life. Jesus' body was broken so we may be healed. The cross of Christ was the altar upon which He would redeem the world from sin. He shed His precious blood as the price for our redemption. To be sure, the blood was not paid to Satan. Jesus' blood was given to His Father for our redemption.

There is such power in Jesus' blood, and only God's blood could break the chains of slavery to sin, disease, and death. Christ's life and His blood defeated death, the grave, and the curse of sin. In Jesus' blood and stripes, we have our healing. Every drop of His blood, every stripe upon His body, brought our healing. Every sickness known to mankind can ultimately find its origin in man. All afflictions were originally birthed when man rejected

God's love, holiness, and presence in the Garden. Yet, by God's grace, we are saved!

We must receive in our hearts that the grace of salvation is both for our soul and our bodies. Jesus commanded that the resurrected Lazarus have the grave clothes removed from his body. Often, we walk as born-again Christians, resurrected in Christ, but with grave clothes covering our beings. You must choose, by faith in Christ, to shed the grave clothes.

The chapters thus far have detailed scriptural accounts of Christ's healing the sick, as well as modern accounts of Christ healing. For what purpose? There is but one answer: that you might believe Jesus is the Christ of God and that in Him alone is life eternal with God. I was once in a meeting in Brazil and I saw an elderly woman walking from the rear of this large church toward me. There were many people gathered around the altar who had come forward to be prayed for. The closer she got to me, I could tell she was having difficulty and was in great pain. The Holy Spirit of God had me to see her through all the people crowded around me. She made it to me and I asked her what it was that she sought of God.

She revealed her ankle to me. And there I saw a large blood clot-looking growth upon her ankle. Just one glance at this infirmity caused my heart to burn with compassion. As I looked upon her, with my heart crying out for her, I asked if I could touch her ankle and pray for her. She agreed. "In the name of Jesus Christ of Nazareth," I cried out to our God for Him to reveal His love and power.

In a matter of few seconds, I removed my hand and God once again demonstrated His great love, mercy, and power. This large growth was gone and all I could see was a little spot. Jesus Christ of Nazareth had delivered her from this affliction. Jesus is still merciful. He's still full of grace, truth, love, compassion, kindness, and power. My heart is that in some small way, this book will help to increase your faith in Jesus because the salvation of your souls and the healing of your bodies is found only in Him. You need not look to any other.

Please, I implore you, believe on Jesus Christ. Receive His love and power into your heart. He truly is the only God that heals you. He heals both the broken heart and the broken body. The apostle John, through the Holy Spirit, penned a mighty verse in his third epistle. He declared, "Beloved, I wish above all things that thou would prosper and be in health even as your soul prospers."

As you read this, I call upon the Lord of Heaven and earth to prosper you in every way; that the Spirit of Christ who is God's *Flame of Love* will keep you in divine health all the days of your life. But please, you cannot become complacent about the One who gave His life for you. You must also stay alert and remain aware of the devil's schemes to keep you unaware of your God and His covenant. If you're reading this, more than likely, you are born again and have been washed with the blood of the cross. Yet it is also possible that you live this life with some old grave clothes on. When Jesus raised Lazarus from the dead, he walked out of the tomb of death. Though he was alive, he was encumbered by the same grave clothes that kept him wrapped in the burial clothing. That was unacceptable to the Lord.

Jesus commanded that the grave clothes be removed from his body. Yes, Lazarus was given life once again by the power of the Holy Spirit. Yes, Jesus has finished His work on the earth. He declared it from the cross: "It is finished." But today and every day, we are to live in the newness of life of both our souls and our bodies. We cannot be content to walk this life wrapped in the grave clothes of fear, doubt, sickness, and despair. The blessings of God await to be revealed in and through your lives, provided we love Him and walk in obedience to His love.

CHAPTER SIX
STUDY QUESTIONS

1) God endlessly loves people, as a result, He heals the non-believer and the believer alike. What is the purpose in God healing non-believers?

___

2) Have you found yourself wearing "grave clothes" in your own life? Practically speaking, what does this look like and how can you shed them?

___

3) God has saved us, yet many people stop there, stuck in grave clothes. What are some of the benefits that go beyond salvation that are available to us as His children?

___

Additional thoughts:

7
HE OPENED NOT HIS MOUTH

If you're a child of God, you are God's own possession. You must never forget His great love for you and your great salvation You must never neglect such a great salvation. His love is truly holy, costly, and more precious than gold. Jesus is worthy and we are to live with a holy love within our hearts burning for Him all the days of our lives. Though even war should rise against us, this we must be confident in, "One thing I desire of the Lord, and that will I seek: that I may dwell in the house of the Lord all the days of my life. To behold His beauty and to inquire in His temple" (see Psalm 27).

In the time of trouble, we must know in our hearts that the Holy Spirit will hide us in His pavilion. This pavilion is the secret place of His heart. There you shall be set upon the rock, Jesus Christ. From the pits of your sickness, disease, or affliction, your head shall be lifted above all the works of the enemy. We shall live singing praises unto the Lord. From this day on, when He says to your heart, "Seek My face," your heart will cry out, "Your face will I seek."

Our God of love and holiness does not want to hide His face from you. It is not His desire to put you or me away in anger. He is your God who helps you, who does not forsake you. He is the God of your salvation. Yet you must cherish and love Him with all your heart above all other loves. You must submit your life each day as a living sacrifice, holy and acceptable in His sight. You must cry out each day, "Teach me Thy way, O Lord, and lead me in a plain path. Deliver me not over into the will of my enemies."

Let us never forget the Word of God declares, "I would have fainted unless I had believed to see the goodness of the Lord in the land of the living" (see Psalm 27). Spend your life in His pavilion. Wait upon the Lord. Be of good courage and He shall strengthen your heart. Wait, I say, on the Lord, receive the reward of the sufferings of Christ at the whipping posts and upon the cross. You must place your heart and reliance upon His love, His stripes, and His name. My prayer is that you will believe His words.

I ask you, to whom is the arm of the Lord revealed? He is despised and rejected of men; a man of sorrows and acquainted with grief. And we hid our faces from Him. He was despised and we esteemed Him not. Surely, He has borne our griefs and carried our sorrows. Yet we did esteem Him stricken and smitten of God. But He was wounded for our transgressions. He was bruised for our iniquities. The chastisement of our peace was upon Him. And with His stripes, we are healed. All we like sheep have gone astray. We have turned everyone to his own way. And the Lord has laid on Him the iniquity of us all. He was oppressed and He was afflicted. And yet He opened not His mouth. He was brought as a lamb to the slaughter. So He opened not His mouth. Yet it pleased the Lord to bruise Him. He had put Him to grief when the Lord made His soul an offering for sin (See Isaiah 53).

CHAPTER SEVEN
STUDY QUESTIONS

1) God's presence is a "pavilion" to us. Have you seen people who neglected this pavilion? What was the result? How do we avoid this?

_____
_____
_____
_____
_____

2) Have you found yourself forgetting the price that was paid to purchase our healing? How can you keep it at the forefront of your remembrance?

_____
_____
_____
_____
_____

3) The chapter describes the price that Jesus paid to claim our healing. What is the significance in Him paying such a high price? How do you navigate this reality as you move forward?

_____
_____
_____
_____
_____

Additional thoughts:

8
JUST LOVE HIM

I remember several years ago when one of our sons was experiencing a most difficult time in his life. He decided to travel and spend some time with sisters at a convent, located in southeastern United States. During that time of seeking the Lord and seeking divine healing for what troubled him, he received the word of comfort that I truly believe impacted His life, and our lives as a family. I want to share it with you.

This was her counsel to him, with tender love, "Just love Him. Just love him." Could it be that we seek the writings of the greatest men and women of God who have moved with the great effect in the gifts of healing and still miss the mark? The Holy Spirit wants you to at least be able to lay this book down and declare one thing: "I just love Him with all my heart." I am convinced that in this place of heart, you will find more than you could ever hope for or imagine. We shall all apprehend the incredible healing, restoration, and power that flows out of the fountain of Jesus' pierced heart.

Every affliction must leave, every sickness be healed, and every torment must flee. But first, each of us has to position ourselves by faith under the fountain of the flow of love found in the blood of Jesus Christ. Without our hearts pierced open by His love, we cannot receive the flow of His love. The key, I believe, is *that* simple counsel given to our son, "Just love Him." Disease, sickness, demonic oppression, deafness, blindness, crippled bodies, even death itself are overcome by the flow of God's holy fountain of living waters and His blood. If just one of you can truly grasp this divine revelation, then I am blessed and will have been successful in the writing of this book.

Please waste no more time searching for a "how to" solution. It's not "how to" but "who," and that "who" is one person: Jesus Christ of Nazareth. My friends, let God's love flood your hearts and live every day giving back to God the only love that He is worthy of—the love He has poured into you. This is how you *just love Him* in that place of heart. In this, you are kept safe from all the works of the enemy, darkness, and evil.

Keep your hope fixed upon Jesus. The Spirit of holiness will keep you pure—spirit, soul, and body.

You ask, "But how can I get to that place?" I hear the words of your Father who loves you: "But we all with unveiled face, beholding as in a mirror the glory of the Lord are being transformed into the same image from glory to glory. Just as from the Lord" (2 Corinthians 3:18). Transformation follows beholding Jesus with unveiled faces. No more forms of godliness. No more pretending. Bring your *real self*. Come broken. Come with a humble heart, with a desperate hungering heart, and simply ask for God's grace to meet you where you are. In your real state of body and soul, ask Jesus to heal you and to change you. It is said, Christianity is not a self-improvement program. It is an exchange of your life for His.

CHAPTER EIGHT
STUDY QUESTIONS

1) The phrase mentioned in the chapter, "Just love Him," is simple yet powerful. What does *loving Him* look like to you?

_____
_____
_____
_____
_____

2) "How to" formulas can create an impersonal and merely transactional view of God. What other negative consequences come when one reduces the gospel to a formula?

_____
_____
_____
_____
_____

3) The chapter implores us to come to God broken. Do we hinder our ability to receive from God by coming to Him pretending to have it all together? How so?

_____
_____
_____
_____
_____

Additional thoughts:

9

HAVE YOU EVER SEEN JESUS?

In the early 1980s, I was diagnosed with a rare bacterial infection caused by me scraping my left knee against some live coral in the Gulf of Mexico. Soon, my knee became very inflamed, infected, and discolored. Following a number of doctor's visits, which included the Mayo Clinic, a culture was taken from my infected area. They were examined and the diagnosis was determined: I had contracted a very rare bacterial infection called Mycobacterium Marinum. Over the following couple of years, this disease required four knee surgeries that left me substantially disabled during that time. It called for a frequent need for crutches, a cane, and even a wheelchair at times.

Those physical limitations actually caused my legs to atrophy. I began to lose muscle mass in my legs. In addition, I was on several different medications that had a very serious side effect on my digestive system. This disease was even treated at that time much the same way you would treat tuberculosis. After those four years of pain, surgeries, and discomfort, I was about to encounter the Lord Jesus' love and power in my own life.

One day, my son Michael, my wife Evelyn, and I were visiting a relative's home. I was seated on the couch in the living room, and I recall my son, Michael, seated on the floor to my right. He was just a young boy. To my left was my wife Evelyn. Normal conversations took place between those that were gathered. But all of a sudden, everything was about to change. A Greek Orthodox priest who had received the baptism of the Holy Spirit entered into the living room. Though I was not saved, I knew there was something truly different about him. I realized it, but I didn't know what it was.

It seemed that God had positioned this priest, my son, my wife, and I for a true miraculous encounter with the Lord Jesus. The priest sat down on a chair opposite me, just a few feet away. I saw that the atmosphere changed. I couldn't explain it, but he looked toward me and he fixed his warm, loving eyes toward mine. He then asked me a question that I will never forget: "Have you ever seen Jesus?"

I was amazed with that question. Yet the power, love, and authority of his words caused me to reply. I said "No, I don't think so." His immediate reply to me was, "Why not?" I just said, "I don't know." He then uttered these words, "Do you want to see Him?" I said, "Yes."

He stood up, came over to me, and grabbed my left knee, which had staples in it and a drainage tube. He squeezed it. Keep in mind, I was wearing pants; he had no way of knowing which knee was infirmed. It was divine. As he grabbed my knee, the pain was beyond description. Yet when he did, I sensed a surge of electricity flowing through my leg and then throughout my entire body. He declared, "In the name of Jesus Christ of Nazareth, be healed." He backed away and said, "Walk to me." I turned to reach for my crutches, but he said, "Stop. You walk to me, and not with the crutches. You walk to me without them."

Keep in mind, I had staples in my legs. My legs were very weak and atrophied, and it was extremely difficult for me to walk without assistance. But in obedience, I stood up and began to take one step after another. My emotions overwhelmed me at that moment. I began to weep. As I walked toward the priest, I realized I had no pain. A day or two later, I returned back to the orthopedic surgeon's office for a routine visit. I was to be scheduled for a year-long aqua therapy treatment. When the nurse examined my leg, she saw that my muscle strength was back to normal, and that my bad leg was actually stronger than my good leg! God had healed me and I wasn't even born again! God healed me and I was not saved. In fact, I would not surrender my life to Jesus' love and lordship for another seven years. But I knew I had encountered the divine, miraculous presence of God and that He had marked me by the Spirit.

CHAPTER NINE
STUDY QUESTIONS

1) We have the ability to let other people see Jesus when we behave like He behaved. How have you seen this play out in your own life?

_____
_____
_____
_____
_____

2) The priest in this story walked in great faith and boldness. What can you learn from the boldness of the priest in this story? How does it inspire you to go forward in healing power?

_____
_____
_____
_____
_____

3) What testimonies can you recall either in your own life or the lives of others that stir up faith within you to see Christ's healing virtue manifest?

_____
_____
_____
_____
_____

Additional thoughts:

10
THE CONCLUSION

My prayer is that as you have read these various testimonies and teachings, somehow the Holy Spirit has imparted the love of Christ deep in your heart. My only desire is that we, as the body of Christ, and whoever might read this book, will come to know that there is an answer. There is a solution. There is a remedy. There's a love that's beyond description that awaits you. This Love has a name: Jesus Christ of Nazareth. He healed my soul as well as my body. To Him alone be all the glory and honor.

His Word is filled with great promises and scriptures that you should confess that reveal the heart, the power, and the compassion of Christ to heal the sick. As I said from the very beginning, this book is not an academic exercise.

My prayer is that *The Healed* has been inspired

by the Holy Spirit. My prayer is that the Holy Spirit, who is the Flame of Love, will ignite your heart and set your heart aflame for Him. That your heart would be branded with the love, power, mercy, grace, and healing virtue of Jesus. I want you to know that Jesus Christ is the Son of God. He came to this earth to destroy the works of the devil, and He has finished His work. He said it Himself at Calvary.

He shed His blood and was crucified on that tree. Yet He rose from the dead three days later, and *He is alive today*. His victory over the work of the devil resulted in His forgiveness of our sins and the healing of our bodies from any disease that would beset us or our loved ones. The Lord only asks one thing of you and me today: that He would be our first love.

The Word repeatedly describes the blessings upon blessings that come to those who love and trust Him. My hope is that as you read this, your heart is stirred, and that you could feel the beautiful hands of Christ placing your heart between His nail scarred hands, almost as in a vice, squeezing you *out of you* and His love *into you*. My prayer is that Jesus will become your first love. Will you do that today? Will you make the Lord Jesus the love of your life?

I know that as you confess His Word over your own life, He will do for you what He did for so many. I remember one woman telling me that she was facing a great trial in her faith. She said, "I felt the love of Jesus in your prayers and His love enveloped me." I pray you too are enveloped in His love. I can recall hundreds of testimonies that I have personally witnessed regarding the healing power of God.

I remember seeing an elderly man who was healed overnight of severe coughing and bleeding in his throat. I remember praying for a young middle school boy who could not read, and I prayed for him, and minutes later he was able to take a history examination, and he scored a B on that test. I remember when my youngest son, Theo, was healed of spinal stenosis. God has touched me so often in so many different ways from my atrophied leg to two other illnesses that I suffered since then. I recall seeing a heroin addict completely delivered; as we returned back to the same church to pray again one year later, I saw him. He had gained fifty pounds and had become a faithful servant of God.

I recall a young man healed of brain damage due to an automobile accident. I witnessed a young woman who was a nude dancer and a prostitute delivered from possession of Satan, and she began to dance and serve God in her church. I remember a young man who had a fused leg, with a steel bar in his leg bent at a 45 degree angle. He was completely healed, and the bar disappeared! A woman with a large tumor on her breast completely healed at a service in Brazil. Another woman in Pakistan whose body was riddled with sores that looked like leprosy. She was prayed for. Then she went into the bathroom to examine herself. When she looked into the mirror, she saw her face was completely clean. She opened up her garments and realized that her entire body was healed!

I remember seeing a young child diagnosed with leukemia in Brazil, who was prayed for. One year later, after we returned, we were told that after our prayer, the parents took the child back to the doctor and the cancer was completely gone. I remember a teenage boy who could not see without glasses was prayed for, and the child instantly could see all the way across a large church without his glasses. I saw a young man diagnosed with an abscess which could not be removed surgically. He could not talk, eat, work, or do much of anything without great pain. Yet within a matter of minutes after prayer, he went into the bathroom and this abscess passed out of his mouth. All the pain was gone, and he was completely healed.

I remember a woman suffering from fibromyalgia that was actually mad at me because I didn't think about praying for her. She approached me after church angry. But she still asked me for prayer. I prayed over her. She went back home and she realized in a matter of days that she was completely healed from fibromyalgia and never again took any pain pills. I remember a young baby in an incubator with a very serious condition, brain issues and heart issues. It was a critical matter. So within a matter of few hours, after we just touched the baby in the incubator and prayed in the name of Jesus, the doctor reported that the child was perfectly normal. Whatever afflictions the child had before we prayed were gone!

I remember a woman that had a cardiac condition who was completely healed and returned back to her doctor and they found no trace of any heart disease. I remember just this past year as we were in Lima, Peru, we were praying for the sick in one of our meetings. The first person we came upon was a man who was very poor and blind. We laid hands upon him, anointed his eyes with oil, and he gained his eyesight!

So what shall I say to you now? Everything I've declared is for the glory of Jesus and for Him alone. The Bible declares that God is no respecter of persons. So, what I say with all my heart is this: what He did for these precious people, He wants to do for you. All He asks is that you call upon His name. You shall realize your healing upon yourself and your loved ones.

What we ask of you is that if you've experienced a healing as a result of Jesus' love revealed in this book, please let us know. If you need healing, please send your prayer requests to us at pastor@jesus-center.us.

May the Lord Jesus Christ reveal Himself to you today and forever. I love you and thank you!

CHAPTER TEN
STUDY QUESTIONS

1) What is the relationship between the love of God and the healing power of God? Why is it important to love people when ministering healing to people?

_____
_____
_____
_____
_____

2) The Word repeatedly describes the blessings upon blessings that come to those who love and trust Him. What sort of blessings have you seen in your own life as a result of trusting Him?

_____
_____
_____
_____
_____

3) The Bible says that God is no respecter of persons. Why is this significant in the realm of healing? What happens when we lose sight of this?

_____
_____
_____
_____
_____

Additional thoughts:

Pastor Theo and his wife Evelyn, have spent the past nearly 30 years, revealing Jesus Christ by the power of the Holy Spirit, to both children and adults, throughout America, Brazil, Greece, Pakistan, India, the Philippines, and other parts of the world. They are the blessed parents of Theo and Michael Koulianos, and six grandchildren. They simply love Jesus with all their hearts and are devoted to seeing the name of the Lord spread abroad, in both word and deed. The Lord has been gracious to them, with His divine confirmation of signs, wonders, healings, and miracles following them; as they continue to this day in teaching the Kingdom of God, preaching the Gospel, and praying for the sick.

Discover more at:

JESUSCENTER.US

TO DISCOVER ADDITIONAL VOLUMES WITHIN THIS
GLOBAL DISCIPLESHIP COURSE, VISIT:

OR

TO CONNECT OR PARTNER WITH THE MINISTRY,
VISIT, CALL OR WRITE TO:

THE JESUS CENTER CHURCH

36750 US HWY 19 NORTH, STE 2051

PALM HARBOR, FLORIDA 34684

PHONE: (727) 412-1432

EMAIL:

GENERAL INFORMATION: *info@jesuscenter.us*

PASTOR THEO: *theo@jesuscenter.us*

EVELYN: *evelyn@jesuscenter.us*

SUGGESTED SCRIPTURE READING

20 PASSAGES ON HEALING

"Heal me, O Lord, and I will be healed; save me and I will be saved, for you are the one I praise."

(Jeremiah 17:14)

"Is anyone among you sick? Let them call the elders of the church to pray over them and anoint them with oil in the name of the Lord. And the prayer offered in faith will make the sick person well; the Lord will raise them up. If they have sinned, they will be forgiven."

(James 5:14-15)

"He said, "If you listen carefully to the LORD your God and do what is right in his eyes, if you pay attention to his commands and keep all his decrees, I will not bring on you any of the diseases I brought on the Egyptians, for I am the LORD, who heals you."

(Exodus 15:26)

"Worship the LORD your God, and his blessing will be on your food and water. I will take away sickness from among you…"
(Exodus 23:25)

"Surely he took up our pain and bore our suffering, yet we considered him punished by God, stricken by him, and afflicted. But he was pierced for our transgressions, he was crushed for our iniquities; the punishment that brought us peace was on him, and by his wounds we are healed."
(Isaiah 53:4-5)

"But I will restore you to health and heal your wounds,' declares the LORD."
(Jeremiah 30:17)

"If my people, who are called by my name, will humble themselves and pray and seek my face and turn from their wicked ways, then I will hear from heaven, and I will forgive their sin and will heal their land. Now my eyes will be open and my ears attentive to the prayers offered in this place."
(2 Chronicles 7:14-15)

"You restored me to health and let me live."
(Isaiah 38:16)

"Nevertheless, I will bring health and healing to it; I will

heal my people and will let them enjoy abundant peace and security."
(Jeremiah 33:6)

"Dear friend, I pray that you may enjoy good health…"
(3 John 1:2)

"He will wipe every tear from their eyes. There will be no more death' or mourning or crying or pain, for the old order of things has passed away."
(Revelation 21:4)

"He heals the brokenhearted and binds up their wounds."
(Psalm 147:3)

"Hearing this, Jesus said to Jairus, 'Don't be afraid; just believe, and she will be healed.'"
(Luke 8:50)

"Heal the sick, raise the dead, cleanse those who have leprosy, drive out demons. Freely you have received; freely give."
(Matthew 10:8)

"But for you who revere my name, the sun of righteousness will rise with healing in its rays. And you will go out and frolic like well-fed calves."
(Malachi 4:2)

"'He himself bore our sins' in his body on the cross, so that we might die to sins and live for righteousness; 'by his wounds you have been healed.'"
 (1 Peter 2:24)

"Heal the sick who are there and tell them, 'The kingdom of God has come near to you.'"
 (Luke 10:9)

"He sent out his word and healed them; he rescued them from the grave."
 (Psalm 107:20)

"Heal me, Lord, and I will be healed…"
 (Jeremiah 17:14)

"…I have heard your prayer and seen your tears; I will heal you…"
 (2 Kings 20:5)

NOTES

NOTES

NOTES

Made in the USA
Columbia, SC
21 May 2020